UNDER THE DARK

JILL BALACKO

Under the Dark
Copyright © 2019 by Jill Balacko

All rights reserved. No part of this publication may be reproduced, distributed, or transmitted in any form or by any means, including photocopying, recording, or other electronic or mechanical methods, without the prior written permission of the author, except in the case of brief quotations embodied in critical reviews and certain other non-commercial uses permitted by copyright law.

tellwell

Tellwell Talent
www.tellwell.ca

ISBN
978-0-2288-1357-6 (Paperback)
978-0-2288-1358-3 (eBook)

This writing is dedicated, with much love, to Bradley.

May 7, 1970 – October 28, 2009

May you rest in peace.

TABLE OF CONTENTS

Introduction 1
A Dream State 3
Way Back When 6
Is there such a thing? 7
A Family Affair 11
The Beginning of the End 13
Not Quite Done Yet 15
A Life Interrupted 17
The What Ifs Can Kill You 20
My World is about to Rock 22
Woulda, Coulda, Shoulda… 24
What Now? 26
Just a Little Crazy… 29
The Years Come and The Years Go 32
Stories from those Left Behind 33
Dear You #2 36
Dear You #3 43
Dear You #4 45
Dear Brad #2 48
Dear Brad #1 52
Take Care of You 55
And so it continues… 56
What you can do for you: available resources for those left behind (survivors) 58
Writing a Therapeutic Letter 61
Suicide in Canada 62

WITH GRATITUDE

As I put the finishing touches on my story, I realize the many people who have encouraged me along my journey. All of you listened and supported me for which I am grateful. You know who you are.

I would like to thank the individuals who contributed their own painful stories. The emotional impact (healing) for you and the reader is greatly beneficial.

With special thanks to Lyn, Naomi, Shelly, and Audrey who read my rough drafts along the way. Without your words of encouragement, I'm not sure this would have been possible. Shelly, I will be forever grateful for the time you put forward in listening, comforting, editing, and sharing what I needed to hear. The completion of this book was made possible by you.

Mom, thank you for shaping me into the woman I have become.

AUTHOR'S NOTE

This story has been told to few. The reasons vary immensely. I want people to understand me and why I am the way that I am. I wanted others to help me figure out why my life has turned out the way it has. My family and friends may be shocked to read this work to learn about the profound way that Brad's suicide impacted my life.

They (whoever they are) tell you that there are always signs. I beg to differ. One might think that the "million miles apart" may have something to do with it, but again, I beg to differ. I have reviewed his emails and letters over and over. I am a professional who has learned about suicide and who has worked with individuals, and their families, following attempted and completed suicides. In the professional world, I know about suicide. I truly believe when I say to someone, "It was not your fault." But when people tell me that same advice, I want to smack them upside the head. It seems like such a stupid thing to say.

(To maintain privacy, some names have been changed.)

INTRODUCTION

When I initially set out to write this story, I had so many ideas. Months turned into years, and I realized that I had to rethink my options several times. The truth is that suicide affects a vast number of people. You only need to research the phrase "suicide in Canada" to discover that ten individuals die by suicide every day. That leaves a staggering number of loved ones (survivors) left behind. As I struggled to deal with my own overwhelming emotions, I soon realized I could not do it on my own. I felt simply alone and confused. As time progressed, all these feelings and thoughts didn't seem to be getting any easier to deal with. I talked to many professionals including psychologists, family and friends, and a local paper in an attempt to reach my goals, including helping others impacted by suicide. My thoughts focused on helping others cope with the loss of a loved one to suicide. I wanted to hear how others coped, and I wanted to share how I coped in an effort to bring such a difficult topic out in the open. The more I talked about it, the more I realized how many people I knew had been impacted by suicide. Talking helped me to hear how others managed to cope.

I decided the best way to help others would be to ask for personal stories of how others have been affected by the death of a loved one by suicide. I wanted to include their journeys as they staggered along the path to find peace. Since the lives of so many people have been touched by the effects of suicide, I thought it would be easy to find others wanting to contribute to this work. The sombre truth is that it is too painful for many to bring up the memories, the hurt and the pain, and all the other emotions associated when a loved one dies by suicide.

I sent out many requests asking others if they wanted to contribute to my book. I reached out to people whom I knew were impacted by the suicide death of a loved one. I stated the purpose would be to help others coping with such a loss. I had many responses, and some people even forwarded my requests to others. I had many people tell me they would love to contribute and even thanked me for supporting such a cause. When the days turned to weeks and the weeks to months, I would reach out once more. The responses I received from people wanting to contribute varied greatly. Some I never heard from again (despite an email or call to check in). Some said that they could not finish their letter as it became too painful. Some stated they had to go seek outside help to deal with the wounds that had been re-opened. Others said that it was just not a good time. I respect every one of their responses. Digging deep within ourselves and openly sharing, what can be such raw emotion, can be exhausting and even debilitating. It can be similar to living the pain and loss all over again. For those people who were able to share their stories and write a letter to that special person for all of us to read, I am forever grateful. Without your words, thoughts, determination and courage, my words would not have the same impact and my sole purpose not possible.

We are not alone in our attempts to understand and find peace. There is no need to suffer in silence.

The reasons for writing this are simple. I want to heal. I want to assist others who are left behind when their loved one dies by suicide. I want to provide hope to those who are contemplating suicide.

A DREAM STATE
SEPTEMBER 2004

I arrive in Las Vegas for, what I term, some much needed me time. There were so many issues in my life that I needed to get away, sort through my thoughts and make some life-altering changes. But, first, I needed a drink.

I make my way through the crowds of the beautiful Mirage casino, find a table by the door and order my Chi-Chi. I am overwhelmed by the loudness of the busy environment. The winning sounds of the slot machines beckon me. While I sit there, trying not to consume my sweet over- priced drink too quickly, I catch a glimpse of someone out of the corner of my eye. The slot machines, the cheers of anticipation and wins, the groans and frustrations of losses, the casino is loud and yet, I now hear nothing. I stare in disbelief as he slowly walks towards me. I gasp.

Can it really be him? My breath escapes me, and I find no words. His thoughts are elsewhere; he doesn't notice me, and he continues to walk past. I catch my breath and whisper his name... "Brad." He is now much too far away to have possibly heard me and yet I notice him hesitating. I hold my breath as he stops, turns, and looks directly into my eyes. With every fibre of my being, I know that he, too, can feel the intensity of the energy between us. He stands there staring at me for what seems like an eternity but in all reality is mere seconds. My heart races. I fear it may explode. He slowly moves towards me, his face expressionless, but I can see it in his eyes - the longing, the desire. I continue to sit, oblivious to my surroundings. I hear nothing. As he nears, he slides one hand into mine and with the other touches my cheek ever so gently. He leans towards me, our eyes lock, no words between us, and he kisses me very softly on the lips. I let out a tiny gasp, my eyes close, and once again I whisper…"Oh Brad."

Within moments I realize I am now standing in an elevator, my hand in his with no words spoken between us; there is no need. He leads me to a beautifully soft-lit room adorned with a wall of windows overlooking the Las Vegas strip. I hear only the beats of my heart and my heavy breaths as they struggle to escape. I lay on the white-laced bed and the soft, white down encompasses my body. The desire between us is incredibly strong. I begin to shake, and I am not sure how long I can handle the pressure. As he leans into me, again he touches my cheek. My pulse quickens, and my desire is mounting throughout my body. He gently takes me into his arms, his eyes never leaving mine. My need for him is insurmountable. I want him, all of him. As the anticipation overwhelms me in ways I never thought possible, I wake up.

The euphoria continues to consume me, and I begin to panic. As I try to slow my heart rate, reality takes its hold. I am at home. My husband Grant snores softly beside me. As tears threaten my eyes, I quietly plead for God to let me fall back asleep. I close my eyes, but sleep eludes me. It's no use. The dream has ended. My heart rate slows, and thoughts of Brad linger. I try to find the reasons for my continual dreams each time, waking up before we share ourselves. My husband stirs, and my guilt absorbs me. I ask myself how I can be lying here with my husband when my thoughts are of Brad. My dreams seem so real and magical. I wonder if Brad ever thinks of me or feels this strong connection that seems to have gripped my life. The more I dream of Brad, the more my thoughts begin to consume me. I know it is inevitable: I will have to re-establish my relationship with Brad. I have no idea how I will make this happen. I ponder the questions: Does he still live in Australia? Is it possible that he still lives at the same address in New South Wales? Maybe his parents still live in the same house? All I know is that I need to find Brad.

WAY BACK WHEN

It all started in 1992, I was working in the small Alberta town of High Prairie. While sitting in a local lounge one evening, a friend recounted when she had travelled to Australia for a year. Her face was alight as she described her adventures. I was sold. I had reached a point where I was no longer content with my life's direction. The next morning, I made a call to the local travel agent inquiring about what was available on a one-year open ticket. She told me of three different travel packages. My response was to book the one that included Hawaii, Australia, New Zealand, and Fiji. The agent appeared surprised at my enthusiasm and the immediacy of my reaction. She questioned whether I was sure that it was what I wanted. I asked her to hurry up and book it before I changed my mind. She had it booked within minutes. Arriving at my job that day, I requested a leave of absence. My request was denied, and I submitted my resignation. Two weeks later, I returned home to Edmonton, Alberta. I hesitantly told my mother that I would be leaving for a year, which resulted in tears from both of us. She was sad and scared while I was excited and scared. I cashed in my provincial pension, packed my backpack and was off to Oahu, Hawaii within weeks.

Hawaii was fantastic! I spent approximately three months there and met a wonderful woman named Melanie. We partied, sang karaoke (well, sort of) and caused a ruckus where we could. Oh, how I miss her! But that's another story for another time.

The Aussies were calling!

IS THERE SUCH A THING?

My next stop was destined to be Cairns, Australia. Little did I know, my life was about to change forever. Although I had only spent three months in Hawaii, I could tell that my financial situation could not support this carefree lifestyle. I knew I had to find employment. Of course, this proved to be a more difficult endeavour than I had anticipated. As the days went by, one thing became certain: a person could make an absolute ton of easy money by selling either vacuums or encyclopedias. As logic set in, it quickly became clear that I would have to support my holiday by selling encyclopedias. Seriously, vacuums would be far too awkward to sell without owning a vehicle! I was going to make easy money selling an item that every household already wanted and needed. I had made a decision, and I was stoked! I couldn't believe my luck.

Well, it was at my first and only daylong training session that I realized I had made a grave mistake. I mean, really, who did I think I was kidding? I couldn't sell an encyclopedia if my life depended on it. One might even ask what the hell I was thinking. My only response to that question is that, well, I guess I wasn't. I do, however, believe in fate. Regardless of whether it was my stupidity or lack of judgment, there I was, ready to learn the ins and outs of door-to- door sales.

My eyes scanned the room to see who else had the same high hopes of earning a fast buck. I was awestruck that I was not the only stupid person there. I knew with certainty that I had to plan my escape. Again, I scanned the room to see if anyone would possibly miss me should I use the loo and make a run for it. It was then, from across the room, that our eyes first met. I couldn't help but notice his beautiful long, blonde hair, blue eyes and that smile. Shortly after, Brad confidently approached me and asked me if I had a vehicle. I assumed he wanted my assistance to get his newly acquired encyclopedias from point A to point B. As I passed judgment, I giggled to myself and thought that at least he had his good looks going for him. I couldn't have been more wrong. As it turned out, he, too, was planning his escape. He had asked if I wanted to join him. His laughter and smile were infectious. We couldn't help laughing as we quickly made a break for it on that exceptionally unprecedented day. I truly can't remember where we ended up that day, but I am quite certain it included beer, gut-wrenching laughter, and some pretty serious conversation. I was hooked! I had never met anyone quite like Brad. He was from New South Wales and was also at a place in his life where he felt a need to get away and discover what life really had to offer. He had placed his guitar in his car and headed west, not knowing where he was going or for how long. We clicked! The hours turned to days, the days to weeks, and the weeks to months. We became inseparable.

We went camping together. We stayed in a tent in the middle of Surfers Paradise, a beautiful seaside resort situated on Queensland's Gold Coast. We also camped at a breathtakingly beautiful and secluded site situated within Byron Bay, located on the shores of New South Wales. Brad played his guitar in the tent while I lay and listened, feeling peace in the world. We fished together. Our day's catch became our pan-fried supper. Brad cooked it with the head still on! Yuk! I did not like that eye watching me! Brad laughed.

Brad loved to surf. He would take me to beautiful beaches. I would sit in the sand and watch him surf. I felt such serenity as I watched him.

There were other adventures, and I loved that he trusted me and let me drive his car.

For Brad's 22nd birthday, I made him a cake shaped like a rabbit. He loved it! Or so he said. Brad had given me a ring to signify an eternity of friendship and love.

We laughed. We cried. We made love on the beach. I can honestly say that those were the best six months of my life.

One calm starry evening while sitting on the beach, Brad played his guitar and sang to me. I believe this was the point when I knew that I had fallen in love. Now, when I hear the Eagles sing "Peaceful Easy Feeling," my eyes well up. I can't help it—that's just how it is. I also can't help but wonder if I would have been a lonely person today if things had taken a different turn.

After a couple months of living life to the fullest in Australia, I realized again that I had to find employment. My money was diminishing. I had nowhere to live and it had become obvious, rather quickly, that I would be spending many more months in Australia. It was through word of mouth that I secured a job washing dishes in a fancy seafood restaurant located on the infamous Fisherman's Wharf. I made a whopping $9.73 an hour, a sum that still astounds me to this day.

After a few, what I call difficult, situations transpired (one of which is a story in itself), I was able to rent a flat with a mate I had met at the restaurant. Once again, things had fallen into place, and my life—nothing short of a miracle. I was so happy! Brad commented on how he loved to be around me because I was the happiest person he had ever met. I have never been as happy as I was at that point in my life.

I turned 25 years old that summer. On my birthday, Brad and I had stayed up all night. A group of four of us went to the beach to watch the sunrise. It looked like heaven, and life was astounding!

A FAMILY AFFAIR

Eventually, it came time to meet his family. Yikes! Now, even if you have never been to Australia, you have likely heard that the majority of the people are nothing short of spectacular. Brad's family proved this to be true. I arrived a few days before Brad as he had also secured employment in Cairns so that he could remain close to me. Although they had never met me, his family took me in and treated me like their own. Thinking back now, I am still amazed at how his mother, father, sister, and brother let this stranger come and live in their home. I think they could tell Brad and I were in love.

When Brad arrived several days later, his parents told us that we needed to sleep in separate rooms. In the end, the protests prevailed. I was permitted to sleep in Brad's room, provided he promised to sleep on the floor. Did he even once keep his promise? Honestly, I cannot recall.

As part of the family, we did many activities together. We went out on their beautiful boat for day trips. On another day, we all drove down the beach in their Jeep. I can remember asking his father to stop the Jeep so I could get out. Several dolphins played in the water. I ran down the beach, mesmerized as they played. I had never seen so many dolphins in the wild. Once again, I felt as though I were in heaven. The family that day was likely wondering if Brad had fallen in love with a lunatic. Within a few short weeks, I felt at home. On one occasion, his mother made a beautiful roast lamb. I even made a meal for the family. I cannot recall what it was, but I remember that it included cheesecake (those who know me know that I absolutely love cheesecake!). While they couldn't believe I had never eaten lamb, I couldn't fathom anyone never having eaten cheesecake.

There were several occasions when I was fortunate to have spent one-on-one time with Brad's mother. One day she took me to the zoo. She made special arrangements for me to enter the enclosure with the koala bears. I had my picture taken with the bears. I still have this picture. What a very special person Brad's mother was to me. She was so kind, caring, and giving. In spite of the years that have passed, I have not forgotten Brad's mother, and the welcoming kindness she showed me during this time. She will forever hold a special place in my heart.

THE BEGINNING OF THE END

As the weeks progressed, a cloud above me darkened. My anxiety increased at the thoughts of having to say goodbye. The sadness was setting in. Brad and I didn't initially speak of what the day would look like when we would have to part ways, but it was inevitable. After seven months, my time was running out, and my stay in Australia was ending. We didn't want this time to end. Brad and I cried weeks before we had to part ways and say goodbye. We entertained many conversations about our future. We didn't know how it could be possible for us to be together for the rest of our lives. The miles between us were vast. It was at this point that Brad had asked to marry me, a drastic measure for what felt like complete desperation between two people. At the time I was thinking that common sense prevailed. But did it? Was it the wrong decision? Either way, I planned to continue with my travels.

The day arrived for me to fly to New Zealand. The thought of that day tightens my chest even now, twenty-two years later. I will never forget that horrid day. I would never have believed that two people could cry as we had. I had found it profoundly difficult to breathe. I think your heart really does break, even a little. That continues to be one of the saddest days of my life. I didn't think I would get over such a love like what I shared with Brad and, perhaps, I never really have. The laughter we shared and the strength in the bond we had had become entangled and was due to be severed. I didn't realize it at the time but, in all likelihood, this was the beginning of the end for Brad and I.

NOT QUITE DONE YET

Although I have dated several men and was married for almost eleven years, I have never felt a love like I had with Brad that summer. Wow! What a profound statement. But as they say, life goes on. Or does it?

After spending time in New Zealand and Fiji, I returned to my life in Canada. I continued to write letters to Brad, his mother, and his sister. We had such a bond between the four of us. I recall reading one of the letters his mother had written me. She informed me that she would no longer be writing to me. This thought breaks my heart all over again.

You see, it was a year after we said goodbye that Brad came to Canada to see me. The times had changed and what had seemed so important to me at one time did not appear to be any longer. Too much time had passed since we said goodbye that dreadful day. Maybe it was the carefree spirit I had while in Australia that was replaced by my work obligations and the need to pay my rent. Perhaps I did not want to feel the pain of having to say goodbye again. I do not know. I cannot say. Something was different, and I became very resistant to allowing Brad back into my life. We spent about a month together before we were able to admit to ourselves that things were not the same. I now realize that it was me who had changed. Brad decided to travel Canada and we parted ways once again. It was at this time that I received the goodbye letter from his mother. I think she felt I betrayed her son. Or is it me who still feels like I betrayed Brad? I think so. I don't know what the hell happened. Our phone calls became fewer, our letters shortened, and our lives had gone their separate ways forever. This was not the case.

I was married in the summer of 1999, approximately five years after Brad and I had parted ways. Life was correcting itself, and I settled down. I married my best friend, a man who made me laugh. I do believe I thought I was happy, and I really was for several years. But as time progressed, I looked back and realized I had settled into a life of complacency. I am not sure when it all changed but in 2002, my sleep became quite irregular. In February of that year, I had crashed my car and it had been written off. Because of my considerable lack of sleep, I had driven head-on into what was, thankfully, a slow-moving lane of traffic. For several seconds after the crash, I had felt a complete sense of peace. Now, I am not a religious person, per se, but, for a brief moment, I believed I had died and gone to heaven. When I regained my sense of reality, I realized that my airbag had deployed. The instantaneous deployment of the airbag caused a flash of white and a dusting of powder, giving me the illusion of the white light that so many speak of in near-death experiences. As awful as it sounds, I was upset when reality had set in and I was, in fact, not at heaven's door. Once again, the course of my life was drastically altered. I never returned to that job as a childcare counsellor, and I took anti-depressants shortly after.

My life felt incomplete.

A LIFE INTERRUPTED

About the middle of 2004, I started having my first dreams of Brad. I still don't understand why or how they happened, but they became more and more graphic until they interfered with my daily living. I tried to brush them off, but they never left. I won't deny it, most of the dreams were profound. Some were very erotic to the extent that I would wake up and have deep guilt. The guilt increased exponentially when I thought of my husband. I felt guilty for something that I was not able to control. I think I didn't want to control the dreams either. Now, when I read back over the journals that I wrote throughout those years, I am both surprised, and yet, not surprised that large percentages of them were writings about Brad. I often questioned whether our relationship had really terminated or if there were adventures for us yet to unfold.

Before my life changed, yet again, I dreamed that Brad's father had passed away. No matter what I did or what I tried to tell myself, I remained disturbed and scared. I had to know that Brad and his family were safe and well. I wrote and rewrote a letter to Brad. It took days to muster the courage to address the envelope. I took a deep breath when I dropped it into the mailbox. It was addressed to the last known address that I could find. Several months later, I received a response. It was from Brad! He had written me back! I remember the feelings I felt at seeing his letter. I was so excited and nervous, my heart rate increased at the anticipation of reading his letter. I found a quiet time and place, settled in, and opened his letter. In his letter, he assured me that he and his family were well. He filled me in on everyone and several of the events that had transpired over the years. No, Brad had never married and no, he hadn't had children. Yes, he still thought of me!

It was great to hear from him. I felt tremendous guilt and part of me still does, as if I was being deceitful. I was married and had a wonderful husband, pets, a beautiful acreage, and a career that I enjoyed. I told myself I wasn't doing anything wrong. After all, we were just old friends getting reacquainted after several years of separation. We had lots to catch up on. Once again, Brad and I became what I can only describe as more deeply connected. The letters became longer and arrived more often. The dreams never went away and sometimes were even more intense. Once again, the guilt I felt at times was overwhelming. And yet, I could not stop the dreams. I even tried to hide the letters that I received from Brad. I am not sure why as it didn't seem to bother my husband that we were writing again. It only bothered me. My husband would say, "Oh, you got another letter from that guy in Australia." I often wonder if my husband chose not to pay attention.

I couldn't wait to read Brad's letters. I would go find a quiet place in the bedroom or read them in the bathtub. We shared things that we were unable to share with others. We talked about how our lives had turned out and how we were disappointed with where we found ourselves. We often wrote about wanting to be happier and we often speculated about the meaning of life. Brad always wrote that he enjoyed the simple life. I was jealous as my life often seemed chaotic and, not at all simple One of the things in my life that brought pleasure was working part-time in the local greenhouse.

I love flowers and had often dreamed of owning my own greenhouse one day. I was not at all surprised to read that Brad owned a yard maintenance and gardening business. He, too, loved flowers. His favourite was the frangipani, (see picture on the outside cover). We emailed one another. He called me Cupcake and Jill Doolie.

The years progressed, and once again things became complicated. I decided at the time and chose, what I now call "The Road Not Travelled."

At some point, and I am not sure when (early 2008), Brad asked me to go to Australia. I couldn't believe what I had read. Even though I told him that I felt stuck in my own life, that I was always wanting more and wrote of my jealousy about the simple life, I was not yet prepared to leave everything I had established at that point. I thought about that letter for weeks and, to this day, I still think about it. I often ask myself what my life would have been like if I had only written different words that day. I get so angry and upset. Yes, I still get resentful towards Brad. But mostly, I am just sad. I am sad at the thoughts of what could have been and will never be. Regardless, I have to accept the words I wrote and the fact that they had hurt Brad.

It was in April of 2009, he emailed me to say he couldn't keep up with our relationship as it had become painful for him. The sadness I felt was deep, but I understood his position. How could I have been so selfish, writing my feelings for him and not taking the next step? It stung. I felt it was only fair for Brad that I discontinue my contact. I had decided, that unless I heard from him first or I was ready to leave my life and enter another one with him, that I would not contact him.

THE WHAT IFS CAN KILL YOU

Although I continued to write letters to Brad, I never put them in the mail. I knew I still had to get my feelings out somehow as they were eating me up inside. Once again, my regrets are infinite. What would have happened if I had mailed them? Maybe he didn't understand how deeply I had felt for him. My questions are endless. Some of the letters I wrote him, but never sent, shared how I felt worried about him and how strange it was that I could feel a connection with him from so far away. I wrote that I all wanted was for him to be happy. I even wrote how I had tried to surprise him by phoning him several times but had never gotten through. I can remember how my body vibrated while I waited for him to answer the phone. What if he had answered? What if he had had an answering machine and I had left a message? I shared my thoughts on how special he was and that no matter what happened, he would always hold a very special place in my heart.

In June of 2009, I wrote, and never sent, a letter stating how I was thinking about him all the time. I wrote that I should go to Australia and see how things might work out for us. I had noted that we were obviously not done with our relationship and that I felt so unsettled about the two of us. Another piece of my heart breaks as I reflect on this now.

I wrote to him about the dreams I still had of him. One dream was me randomly showing up on his doorstep. I shared how happy he was to see me. In one dream I learned I could fly. I had flown to Brad's house and convinced him that if he held my hand we could fly together. We flew around Australia that night. After I had taken him home, he had informed me that he didn't like me anymore. When I awoke from this dream, I quickly checked my emails as I was sure he must have felt…something…from across the seas. There was nothing. I felt such disappointment. In my letters, I asked if he had found normalcy in his life and if he had figured out the meaning of life. Little did I know, he was suffering his own battles.

MY WORLD IS ABOUT TO ROCK

And then it happened in December of 2009. I had driven to Saskatoon, Saskatchewan for three days of employment training. During the drive, Brad consumed my thoughts. The entire three days encompassed absolutely nothing but thoughts of Brad. I don't recall the purpose of the training. During the long drive home, I had made up my mind. I was prepared to leave my life in Edmonton. I had a strong need and desire to meet up with Brad and to see where our lives could take us. I felt exhilarated. I was also relieved, as though a lifetime of weight had been lifted from my shoulders. I couldn't wait to email Brad and tell him I wanted to come and be with him. In contemplation of my email, I decided to write a draft of what I was going to say to him. I did not want to say the wrong things but I knew, with all my heart, that I had to share my true, honest feelings with him. Here is a rough draft of the email, December 3, 2009.

I was on my way to Saskatoon for a course. Before I was 30 km down the road, I thought of you. It has been months since I heard from you—I wonder what you are doing and if things are working out with the new girl you started to date. I want you to be happy, but I know deep down inside I want you to wait for me. I think about you so often. I wonder what life with you could be like. You own a garden business for crying out loud. It seems like a dream for me to work with you in a gardening business. There must be a reason you never married. *There must be a reason neither of us has children. I wonder if you still think of me or if you are missing me. What would you do if I showed up at your door? I have dreamed of meeting you in so many places—sometimes you walk past me in anger and sometimes you just come to me. Oh Brad, why are you on my mind so much? There must be a reason—we can't be done yet. I spent three days thinking of you and feeling guilty. Why am I not happy at home? I have so much and yet my thoughts turn to you. All the way home my thoughts continued to be of you. Every song I hear—the people I see—I need to talk to you and yes, I realize, that I need to see you. I am willing to bear the consequences so that I can see you and hope we can either pursue a relationship or I can get on with my life. I have decided that we should meet somewhere. Perhaps the States, while I am on leave with income averaging. I hope you agree to meet me. I can't keep wondering woulda, coulda, shoulda. My feelings for you are so strong that they are interfering with my life I have here. I now believe that we must meet. I am not sure what to tell my husband. I love him, and I don't want to hurt him, but I feel I am hurting him, myself, and you by not being honest about how I feel. Perhaps I can go away for a week, meet you and then decide what to do from there. For some reason, you and I are not done yet. I am going to email you tomorrow, from work and ask you if you would consider meeting me in February. Somehow, I have to deal with my feelings. Dreaming about you and thinking about you so much is not helping me in my life. I have made a decision, but I am also very scared. Scared of what you will say and scared of losing my husband and the life I have established here. I will have to trust my instincts and hope they are not steering me wrong.*

WOULDA, COULDA, SHOULDA…

I had finally made a decision regarding the direction of my life. I got to work the next morning with every intention of sending Brad the email. As luck would have it, my absence had created a backlog of work. I was unable to send the carefully constructed email explaining my excitement to Brad. I decided it would have to wait until that night or the next day when I returned to work. I felt relief as I drove home from work that day. When I arrived home that afternoon, my husband informed me that I had received a letter from Australia and that it was on the coffee table. My heart rate immediately increased, and I felt as though I might suffocate and not make it to the coffee table. I was in awe. I knew without a doubt that Brad had felt the intensity of my thoughts and feelings the past couple months. He was writing to ask me when I would be arriving in Australia. When I got to the coffee table, I felt a wave of unease go through me when I recognized the handwriting. It was not Brad's. It was his mother's. My immediate thoughts were that she was writing to give me shit for upsetting Brad a couple months before. I thought that it would be okay now as I was prepared to make it all right and go be with him. We had the rest of our lives to be together. Her letter was postmarked November 22, 2009.

Dear Jill,

This is a very sad letter, but I thought I should write and let you know that Bradley died on the 28th of October. We are all devastated as you must be at reading this. Bradley was suffering very badly from deep depression. He was hospitalized twice during the last three weeks of life. They let him out of hospital saying, "There is nothing more we can do." He was just a lost soul. We cared for him most of the time during the past 3 months, trying to bring him out of his depression. He hung himself, Jill, 4 days after leaving hospital. I can't tell you how we miss our beautiful, gentle son. Our hearts are broken. We loved him so much, and we tried so much to help him. He will be in all our hearts forever. Write to me if you like, Jill.

Love from "Brad's Mom"

Everything around me crumbled. My life was devastated, never to be the same.

WHAT NOW?

Over the years, I have kept some documentation of my thoughts, my questions, and my feelings regarding his death. Even being four years later, I still become overwhelmed and break down in tears. Today, as I write this, the tears flow. To describe my feelings right now is overwhelming— disbelief, guilt, shame, frustration, sadness, broken, anger towards myself and Brad, loneliness, and the list goes on. Like a tornado, the emotions consume me, disrupting my balance and igniting a sense of devastation. The following is a list of some of the thoughts, feelings, and emotions I have documented throughout the years.

> *I see you in every song I hear such as "I'm going home" and "I imagine you with me with everything I do."*
>
> *I see you in other people I see—Kaylen Porter, Seinfeld, Michael Jackson, the kid at the farmers market who was playing the guitar.*
>
> *I see you every time I go to the beach or watch surfers.*
>
> *I ask myself what if you would have answered the phone one of those times I called—I had come to see you—you had told me you were hurting so much— your mom had told me you were hurting—I had sent one or any of my letters—I didn't stop emailing*

> *you—I had spent more time when you came to Canada—I was more honest with how I was feeling?*

I continued to write to Brad even after I had been informed of his death. Here are some of the entries:

> *I'm so angry at you, I miss you, I hate you, I love you...why, Brad, why?*
>
> *Are you watching over me? Can you feel how I hurt inside? Can you see the pain in my eyes? My life is forever changed.*
>
> *How can it be? Why, Brad? It's been 4 months since I found out, and I still can't quit crying. I thought we could be together one day. You said you were going to teach me how to surf. I don't want to believe your mother. I want to email you, and I want you to email me back.*
>
> *I want to see you, you bastard! How could you take these dreams away from me? Why didn't you tell me? Your letters were always so wonderful. You were always doing so much and being so busy. You wrote such beautiful things to me. Were you lying?*

I remember thinking how I had misjudged Bradley's mother, and how she must be one sick woman. You see, I had hoped that her letter was not true and that Brad had not killed himself. I hoped maybe she faked her own son's death to see how much I really loved him. I thought it would have been more appropriate if she had just asked me how I felt rather than devising such an elaborate plan. And yes, I did email him to see if he would respond. He didn't.

One of the entries in my journal reads:

> *Oh Jill, I hope you don't blame yourself? Of course, that is what I would say to you. But, how do I not? The last communication we had was him being angry at me. Why didn't I do more? Why didn't I write? Why didn't I email? Why didn't I try to call? I thought about him constantly and yet I didn't want to hurt him until I was sure I could give more. I had no idea how much he was hurting. The whys and what ifs are going to kill me.*

JUST A LITTLE CRAZY...

I find it amazing to see what lengths people will reach to find peace. A couple of examples for me are when I went with my friend in early 2012 to see a psychic in downtown Edmonton. The psychic quickly informed me that Brad was stuck between two worlds. The psychic used the example of a fly being locked between two panes of glass. He went on to explain that some people call this purgatory. Again, I state that I was never seriously dedicated to any particular religion, but I had heard, from somewhere, that people who choose to die by suicide go to hell. This psychic told me that I could help Brad pass through so that he would no longer be struggling. He suggested that I might want to get in touch with a medium to assist Brad with his journey. I was devastated yet again. I didn't know whether to believe this or chalk it up to entertainment (not very good entertainment at that!).

On February 2, 2012, I was brave enough to contact a well-known medium named Laura. It was an experience I shall never forget.

Before seeing her, I had quietly asked Brad to be there with me. Call me crazy, but I do believe that since his death, he has been around me. I believe I feel his presence at times. On more than one occasion, I have had what can only be described as a weird experiences. They mostly occur around significant dates such as Christmas and birthdays. One time I let my cat outside. I was vacuuming when I felt what I can only describe as a strong presence in the house. I felt hot and then cold. I looked up to see cat staring at me, with big eyes, from under the kitchen table. I have no way to explain how she got in the house. There were incidents with lights flickering, and then there was a time when a very unyielding door had closed on its own. These occurrences used to send shivers down my spine and cause the hairs on my neck to stand at attention. Now I welcome them. I hoped that Laura, the medium, could assist me in establishing communication with Brad.

As I walked into her home and sat down, she quickly told me that he practically walked in with me. She said that he wanted to tell me that he was okay and that I, too, would be okay one day. My cheek warmed, and she said he had just kissed me. I was obviously emotional, and when I said that I was really angry at him, he said it was okay for me to be angry and that he wanted me to know he was not angry with me. As I cried, she informed me that Brad said he had gone too soon and that he didn't realize all the pain he would cause. Laura told me she had to tell Brad to slow down because he had so much to share with me. She said he was definitely a writer in his life. She explained how he said he was fine and was not lonely as his grandmother was with him. I remembered his stories about Grandma Jean. (I wish I would have met her.) Laura stated that Brad mentioned that what he did (suicide) was in no way my fault and that he had thought about it before doing it. There was a mention of the number five to which I could not relate, and he communicated a few more things. I was left with feelings of relief and utter exhaustion. Part of me felt the loss all over again. The anger and sadness pained me. I was grateful for what Laura provided that day. I believe that he did share with me, and I hope that we will continue to communicate with one another for eternity. Perhaps my grief and loss can turn into a sense of peace and calmness. Following my meeting with Laura, I wrote:

Although tragic, Brad's death was pivotal in the turning of my life. I would like to think that we could have been together, but I guess we will never know what could have been. I know now that he is okay where he is and that he is not angry with me. That alone is comforting and if I can count on him to visit me "over here" every now and then, then I will continue my healing journey.

I would never be going to South Africa for seven weeks to fulfill one of my life-long dreams. Who knows, without Brad, I may still have been in a marriage that offered contentment and Less happiness as time progressed. I have to find the silver lining in this if I am to heal completely. I do not believe that will ever be possible; the loss has been devastating.

Although Laura brought up Brad's mother, as he had mentioned her, the comments that I heard that day were too hurtful and painful for me to share here. She knows how she feels. Should she read this, I pray that his mother was successful in her efforts to replace anger and blame with peace and calmness. I also wish for to her to believe that, yes, Brad is indeed okay now.

I wrote a letter to Brad after I met with Laura:

Thank you, Brad, for coming to me and providing me with some peace in my life. Brad, I will love you always. Rest well, my friend, and may peace be with you. And yes, you can sit on the edge of my bed any time you like! Well, maybe not any time, you know what I mean!

THE YEARS COME AND THE YEARS GO

It is now June of 2014, and many things have happened that contributed to my inability to complete this book sooner. Although I have thought about putting the effort to complete it often, I had not been in the proper headspace until now.

During the final edits, I found myself in tears all over again. Last week, the day before my birthday, I believe that Brad made his presence known again. It was very early morning, and I believe I was still dreaming. However, the physical and emotional sensations remain with me, still fresh. I was lying in bed, the lights were out, and the door slightly ajar. I felt something different. I watched as the bedroom door quietly and slowly almost closed. The room temperature increased, and my body temperature rose significantly. I felt a presence move all around my bed before feeling a pressure pushing my body ever so slightly into the mattress. I reached out to touch him as I was sure he was lying beside me. Brad? Are you really here? Did I feel him? I think so.

Perhaps on some level, I didn't want the closure and that was part of the hesitation.

STORIES FROM THOSE LEFT BEHIND

I hope that the following unedited stories and letters will be as helpful and supportive to you, the reader, as they were to the individuals who wrote them. These are their letters.

DEAR YOU #1

Dear Dad,

April 17, 1997…shock, grief, denial, disbelief, confusion, horror, abandonment, realization, fear, selfishness, anger, guilt, and even hate. This was the order of my emotions when I was told that you had committed suicide. I didn't know I could experience that many different feelings in a matter of minutes, but that's what happened. Shock, grief and denial, all understandable…but the disbelief for me, was all about the when and how. You were 72 years old, and you jumped out of your 7-story apartment window. How do you live for that long, and then choose to die that way? You took pills for depression all your life, so why not just overdose? And then came my horror…did you change your mind on the way down, but it was too late?? How could you do such a thing to your kids? How could you leave us like that? You're never coming back. You're never coming back. You're never coming back!! What are we going to do without you here? Why the hell did you have to leave us?!! Why couldn't you just relax and enjoy life? What did we do to make you leave? what did I do to make you leave? Why didn't I talk to you more the last time you were here? Why didn't I understand you more? Why wasn't I nicer to you? Why didn't I help you more? Why did I make you take that shock treatment? Whywhywhywhywhywhywhywhy??? Oh, how I hate you for making me feel this way…But how can I love someone, and hate them at the same time? People called suicide selfish and that's what I was thinking about you. So, when people asked how you died, and I told them suicide, and I could see the pity, and they wouldn't look me in the eye, then it turned into embarrassment. The stigma of suicide, that's what keeps us all from telling people, because no one really gets it. No one really knows that you weren't being selfish, and they don't want to know. What do I think now? It was probably the most courageous thing I've known anyone to do, even though it hurt me terribly. Having you here all these years would have been wonderful, but making you stay, knowing how much pain you were in…that would have been selfish…on my part, not yours. Your granddaughter's principal was the only person who, when I told her what happened, looked at me and asked, "How long did he suffer from depression?" Only one person understood…in 17 years.

I still have the same feelings, that's never going to change. I don't hurt as much now, because I understand more about your depression, but I still cried writing this, because you've missed out on so much. That's the part that bothers me the most…you left before you could see how all of our lives turned out. I lost mom when I was 17, so you were the only one here to see my good times and bad…you weren't here to see your granddaughter grow up into an amazing young woman or see your great-grandson be born and watch his amazing football throws. It's so sad that you couldn't be here to witness everything yourself. And, what I do hate, is that a disease was what forced you to make that choice.

Everyone will deal with suicide differently, I suppose, because the way their loved one chooses to leave could be different from yours, but I believe the emotions will be the same. Maybe they'll just be dealt with in a different order. I would tell people to do just that...deal with them. I bottled everything up, thinking all along that I needed to be strong for your granddaughter, but because I didn't talk about it, neither did she, and we've both suffered the consequences.

Years later, when I could look at your eulogy, I also found a poem of your choice, that was read at your funeral, called I'm Free. It opened my eyes to the pain you were suffering, and the unimaginable thoughts that you must have dealt with every day...I'm so sorry that I didn't learn more and recognize more...I'm sorry that it took me so long to understand...I'm just so sorry that you had to leave...

Shelly

DEAR YOU #2

Dear readers,

I continue to evolve in my relationships, mental health issues, and how I move in society and given this assignment, have come into an even deeper understanding of what the trauma of a death by suicide or attempts at death by suicide can have on those left to live without a loved one or with the threat of attempts to die. I am known to be quite candid about discussing a cousin's death by suicide, and my brother's death by suicide. One will also hear me talk about my sister's death by suicide several times and when she was brought back to life. There is great contemplation about my other brother who endured a long recovery after a near-fatal vehicle accident when a drunk driver hit him and his slow death by physical ailments and alcohol abuse. His comment, "if you had this much pain, you would drink too." Where does my candidness come from, my resiliency? This all comes full circle, from the beginning of education about mental health and breaking the stigma associated with, and my interest in society as a kid. I started volunteering at a crisis suicide line directly out of high school and pursued a career in policing/correctional services. In fact, when my brother completed his death by suicide and my sister's attempts followed, my other two brothers asked me what was wrong with me because I did not see the "signs" because I was working at the crisis centre. My resiliency came from anger—the injustice—guilt, but mostly from my mother who had such a veracious love for her children and God. She expressed her sorrow about the death of her children and that she thought of them every day as if their death was the day before. Despite this, she continued to be present in a joyful, loving, and hopeful manner and is perceived as an angel and an example that faith and gratefulness are very important to healing and living a good life. Many times, I would advise her that the churches practice to bury those children not baptized or who had ended their life by suicide, outside church perimeters, as barbaric and not relevant to changing beliefs. Her infant daughter eventually was moved to the main cemetery. Cremation was also something unknown to my mother's ancestry and it added to her grief that my brother's remains would not be in the family cemetery. After much deliberation, with flashlights and new sod, we buried the empty urn alongside my father's graveside as she felt the vessel needed to also be returned to the earth. Many years later when my other brother died, we had to pull up the sod again and put his empty urn in there and although it was funny, there was a real peace that this brought to my mother. This story traverses over the year 1940 and into today.

Education and understanding save lives. Sometimes, one of my nieces, an adult with a family now, is overwhelmed with gratitude for being alive and loving, and she randomly calls me to thank me for being the one she could call before she completed the task to die by suicide. My children may get tired with me if I am checking in with them for their mental well-being, but I know because of it, they have saved their friends' lives, they have said "Mama, I think I am depressed." So, the full circle has manifested itself into my movement to educate those around me. I am selfishly not wanting to have to mourn the loss of a child or loved one. One person at a time, and this is all of eternal significance.

Dear brother,

Our mother always spoke of the death of each of her children x 3 with deep grief and told us that the loss feels like it happened yesterday. Many years later, one of your children would tell me "I think of my Dad, every day "and it jolted me to think that each of your children who had found you in death, also felt the same loss as if it was yesterday. It has been that fear for myself that has propelled me to advocate for mental wellness and mental illness, fear that I would suffer the loss of someone dear to me and when I became a mother, my own child, and fear that I might miss something.

There is a sadness in reading Mom's diary as she describes the RCMP officer coming out to the farm and telling them the news, and she did not use the words death by suicide. There is sadness in knowing that we attended a service and my parents drove back to the farm, and we drove to our cities and jobs. I perceived our parents as not having a supportive and loving marriage equipped with the tools to manage the grief and weight of losing a child and what followed later was explicit grief in not understanding why you would have taken your own life.

I did not know you well, brother. I was born 10 years after the rest of you and did not partake in the tough times of the pioneer living, and, therefore, you had a unique bond with one another. I always felt I lived on the periphery, removed by age from something that was extra special. Our mother told me in her journal that she was puzzled that you had not joined us for our large family get-together and continued to call you that weekend. We all learned after the fact that when the children walked into the garage that they were the first on the scene and their lives changed forever. It was after the service that I would come to know that you had been estranged from your wife, separated and living away from home and that you had chosen to return to the family home to die by suicide. I also learned that you had given many possessions away and visited all the other siblings except me.

These visits were all perceived by the others as a last visit of goodbye. I was not close to you and lived farther away. I did not deserve my other grief-stricken brother's anger that I had failed the family by not being able to predict your actions, and I felt further alienated from the family. I am embarrassed to say that I felt shame for not feeling loss or sadness or missing you, anger at the loss and sadness it caused your family, and parents. In the 1980s suicide prevention education included signs of suicide and that has now evolved into changes in behavior and symptoms of mental illness and that one may not see changes in behavior and still always, it is not anyone's fault if the result is still death by suicide. I felt guilty for a long time that maybe my siblings were correct, not only did I not personally miss you, I may have missed the signs, and if my siblings thought that, did my parents feel the same way? Our mother had a fast and furious steadfast faith in God that kept her solid, feeling not alone, and with hope that she would see you in heaven, including her beloved pets(I told her church could go to hell, of course, pet souls go to heaven). She loved you sooooooooo much and her mourning is part of her legacy of love and is the cornerstone to my own parenting.

Your children and your wife have always told me that they appreciated that I was one of the only family members to contact them, write, and make an effort to see them. It took me many years to understand that there were family members that blamed your marital difficulties and wife for your choice to end your life. Your mother referred to your wife as (she) for a period of time in her journaling. There was what I refer to as DIVORCE by DEATH, and this blaming and judgment resulted in your children being abandoned by extended family. They needed the cousins that were the same age to play with, the presence of unconditional love by grandparents, and they were almost shunned by the lack of understanding and response to grief. I had spoken many times to your mother to help her understand mental illness and your actions, and she always told me that she regrets that you could not tell someone how bad it was. I know that each of your children has had to deal with this trauma and will do so for the remainder of their days. The mother of your children continued to do her best and persevered to maintain relationships in the family. It was not until I divorced and struggled as a single parent that I could understand her at a different level and remark on how courageous she was to handle this trauma and continue to parent. I am sad that you cannot see who they have become and spend time with your grandchildren.

So, I know that you were close to our cousin in friendship and age and that her death by suicide was traumatic and a huge loss. As young children, I recall meeting with the other cousins and going to that same water well (the site of her death). Even as I think about it, I can smell the water well, the rope, and hear the sound of the bucket as it travelled down to the water. As children, we were just curious and talked to each other as no one else talked about it. Your mother writes in her journal how she used to have to make you safe in the one-room house in the winter while she went outside, descended by ladder into the water well, and broke the ice on the top to bring water up. She wondered what would happen to you if anything happened to her. She also talked about her niece's suicide as if this young woman, too, were her own child. I was part of many discussions with her to explain about postpartum depression. You know that this niece left an infant and that this tragedy meant that my aunt and uncle would not know this grandchild. There were family feuds, and my aunt was never the same, not providing the nurturing and parenting for the other surviving children and became estranged from her family.

I cannot imagine having to survive this tragedy. Mom never understood this and continued to try to make contact. Your aunt passed away this year, and I had a peace with it as I felt that, finally, she would be able to see her child in spirit, and I came to understand how differently our families dealt with suicide. I wonder if you thought about her when you made your decision, and I want you to know that your mom would have asked you all the questions. She would have informed you.

She would have tried to help if she had the knowledge, if society had the knowledge at the time. Mom learned a lot about mental illness but after the facts. I think that Mom benefited from the support and education over time and came to understand the effect of trauma on family. Even as I edit this, months after it was written, I am remorseful for lingering flashes of anger at my aunt for abandoning her family, at you, and for members of our family in their reactions to their loss. How can we fault others if we simply do not know?

Dear brother, your siblings grieved greatly for you. The sister that was closest to you and our cousin suffered from mental illness before that and struggled at times. After you left this earth, one brother has never worn anything but black to this day, and the sister tried several times to die by suicide and was resuscitated each time. "Wake up" was what my brother said as my sister had been visiting me and, again, according to them, I was responsible for not preventing this. I do not need to write her a letter. Our discussions have helped me to see where the mind goes when ready to die by suicide, or where any of our minds go when mentally ill, when it feels so very alone, so full of anguish and no hope. I am grateful she is still alive and that our dear mother did not have to endure that grief as well. Forgive us who mourned or did not, and for those of us who partook in the unfair crusade against anyone who hurt you so bad you felt that death was your only choice. Forgive us as we did not know you were suffering and needed support. It has taken decades to come to a different understanding about your suicide, and there are gifts that followed this tragedy. This fueled my parenting efforts so that there are no secrets, that feelings are okay, crying is okay. There is always an age-appropriate explanation for my behavior, for life and death. It has helped to keep my children understanding and in the loop that things are not their fault and that they are loved and supported when experiencing stress or loss. My children have always been heard and are perceptive to others needing support and comfort. The greatest comfort is seeing them loving to one another, kind to others. It can be that simple today. I know your children have gone for help. It can be as simple as telling someone how you feel today. I am appreciative of being able to listen and hope for peace in each of us. So, with that dear brother, go in peace, and I hope you are laughing and full of understanding and love because that is of eternal significance.

You are still my brother. With love, your sister.

DEAR YOU #3

Dear Dad,

I have thought about this letter for a while now. I imagined what I might say and how to get the words out. I sit here crying as I have so many thoughts and feelings. There are many reasons for my overwhelming feelings of sadness. I can't imagine you thinking you were an inconvenience. Those words really hurt when I read them, and I really wish you hadn't felt that way. I never, in a million years, thought this was how things would turn out. I always thought you were so strong and now I think you must have been so sad, scared and lonely. I can't even imagine and, honestly, it's even painful to think about. Everything happened so fast. I thought you were feeling better and yet I wonder if part of me knew you weren't. I think about things you said, and I wonder if I should have said or done things differently. Were you trying to tell me something, and I wasn't listening? I'm so sorry they put you in a hospital room with such an ill gentleman. Is that when you decided? I blame the hospital and think that that never should have happened. I realize that is my anger at feeling helpless about all this. I guess I need to blame someone. You had so many friends that cared for you and thought the world of you. Why didn't you at least wait to see what the Dr. had to say? I think you could have had a lot more good times yet. But maybe that's selfish of me? Is it wrong for me not to blame you? I don't, really. Maybe I do, I just don't know. You were such an independent man and you seemed content. But I guess you were not happy in the end. I have guilt. I hope you did not live your life for us kids. You seemed to live life so simply. I hope that was the way you wanted to live and not the way you felt you had to. You have done so many amazing things in your lifetime. I was so proud to hear how you taught the children about rocks and minerals. How did I not know you went into schools and did that? Either way, it makes me proud of you.

It scares me when I wonder if you were scared in the end. I recently received the coroner's report and it stated you yelled for help. Did you change your mind in those last few seconds of your life? Did you decide you wanted to live but it was too late? "They" tried to save your life, but indeed, it was too late. Did you feel at peace? Were you lonely? Was it painful? I don't want to know you suffered. I saw the newspaper report and it will be forever etched in my memory. You looked so alone and for that, I am so very sorry!

I hope I wasn't a disappointment to you. I only ever wanted to hear you say you were proud of me. In the end, I am grateful because two of your friends said you were. That helped me to feel better.

I am so grateful your friend called us and that I got to hug you, say goodbye and tell you that I loved you. I am not sure how I would have managed with this had I not had that opportunity.

Part of me is glad you are not suffering and part of me wishes you would have waited for your appointment. I guess that's neither here nor there. I hope that "big rug in the sky" is peaceful for you. Rest well knowing that you touched so many lives, inspired so many people and are thought of so fondly by so many.

I love you! Me

(P.S. You even put the seats in the car…)

DEAR YOU #4

To whoever is feeling the pain and loss of someone who has died by suicide. This is my story:

My father decided to leave this world on November 8, 2003. Although he had tried on a few occasions, it still took me by surprise. A cry for help is one thing, right? But when it actually happens, a part of you dies inside. What could I have done? I wish I could take those words back, etc., etc. I am here to talk to you through the wall of pain and tell you that nothing, no words can stop someone who has made that decision.

Let me pause in my letter to describe my suicide attempt when I was only 16. I can tell you, that when someone has made that decision, it has not come easy. I can only tell you what I felt. There are no consultations, no one else is responsible. I had made friends with the darkness. I was lost, I didn't know why I was so "fucked up" or why my family was. I was tired of hanging out and talking with the "normals." The pain, its origins a mystery until my adulthood, would become unbearable. In the darkness I sat, it being my only friend. The darkness encompassed me, and I welcomed it. My choice was not a reflection of anyone or anything around me. This would end the pain. And yet, no success. For that, I am glad.

The pain and sorrow you feel because not only have you lost a loved one, but there are so many questions and no answers. But like I said before—there are no answers. It is not about you or anything anyone did. It is not about a last fight or those last words you said. The choice had been brewing long before that and it had nothing to do with you. Do not think this person was selfish either. It is a conscious choice and usually, mental illness plays a part in that choice. "If only I had gotten them some help!" We can only live our lives with what we have been given. If a person chooses to get help, again that is their choice. My father got help but maybe it was too late. I have to respect that my father chose to leave us this way. You will think this cold and unfeeling, but my father's suicide set me free. Once I pulled myself out of the pity, the anger, the angst and the rage I looked in the mirror, saw my father and decided I would not go there again. I packed up my things and left my husband. I got therapy…lots and lots of therapy. Get it where you can. I got metaphysical counselling, psychological counselling, EMDR therapy (where I remembered the childhood trauma). Talk to people, there is no shame here—the decision was never yours. Join a group, do whatever it takes to lift you out of the darkness.

This will not happen overnight. It took me years of grief, of tears and rage, and yet I made it. I made it through the darkness, and you will too. Cry all you can, write all you can, talk all you can as often as you can. The pain will subside. Think of it this way. When you were born, you were given a nice wool sweater to wear for this life. Whenever you have trauma, you get a little tar stain on the sweater and when you heal that trauma, you can remove that little piece of tar.

Of course, it will always leave some fuzz. And when a loved one leaves by choice, it is like someone has dipped the sleeve of your sweater into tar. Take some time to cry and rage, the tar will harden, it will be easier to get it off. But go and talk to people, because if you don't that sleeve will stretch from the weight of the tar and trip you up. Talk and talk and pick that tar off bit by bit. Learn to love the fuzz it leaves behind; you've earned that fuzz.

Most of all, keep going. Keep going to work, keep walking, keep talking, keep living.

Nathalie

DEAR BRAD #2

(I am including this note to inform the reader that I had, in fact, written a previous letter that I found many months after writing this one. It follows this one.)

August 31, 2017

Dear "Bradely,"

It's been about an hour now since I knew tonight was the night for this to finally happen. I haven't quit crying since. I just can't believe that after all these years my heart can still feel so broken. I know I have been somewhat emotional lately, but I haven't allowed myself to feel this for a long, long time. Part of me feels like a hypocrite, but I just didn't realize that I had never written a letter, to you, about… well, everything about your death. **I** *have spent so many years asking so many people to write letters to their loved ones and it took my friend/doctor of psychology/initial editor to end her curiosity by asking me, where in my book my letter to you was. I spent so much time and effort asking so many people, and I had never even written one to you. Not only did I block it out for eight years, but it's been months since she pointed it out to me. Now I know why it has taken me all this time. I think I always knew why, but now I am actually feeling it.*

Brad, I miss you! I never got the chance to talk to you or say goodbye. It's like our story never got a chance to be complete, it just ended. I hope this will help me to complete more of it. I think I tricked myself into believing I dealt with more of it than I had. I've told our story to several people now, not realizing until recently how much effect your death still has over me. I feel bad, but I still find myself getting really angry at you. Here I am, 50 years old and still by myself.

There are days I feel so lonely, and I get more angry because of all the "what ifs" that go through my mind. What if you didn't end your own life? What if, like my friend says, you had held on for just one more minute? What if I'd figured it out sooner? What if you would have told me the pain you were in? What if I had gone to Australia? What if we had a gardening company together? What if we had lunches on the beach? What if we had a nice small house in the country? What if you were here to hold me now and tell me everything was going to be okay? Woulda, Coulda, Shoulda…didn't! Today I taught the lesson on "radical acceptance." Perhaps this is why this is happening today. I talked about how the pain of losing a loved one can turn to prolonged suffering if you don't deal with the pain and accept it. Perhaps I have kept more in than I care to realize. I know I have to forgive you for what you did, and I know I have to forgive myself for not trying sooner. Sometimes, I think I have and then something like this happens, and I feel like I've taken several steps back. I wish you would have let me know how bad things had gotten for you. I wish you would have given me the chance to be there with you. Maybe, just maybe, I could have helped. Maybe I should have realized things sooner. Maybe if I had mailed the letters I wrote to you and maybe if I'd have tried to call you sooner or more often. Maybe, maybe, maybe. Brad, I didn't, and I am so sorry! I'm sorry I let things go, and I am sorry I wasn't there for you when you needed me. One of the few things in my life that I will forever regret. Unfinished business. I don't feel like our story every got the chance to play out. Neither one of us was fair to the other. It really is true that life isn't fair sometimes. I hope that as I write this and finish up the book of our story that I will be able to find myself forgiving us both. I believed the psychic when she told me you told her you didn't realize how much pain this would cause for so many. I hope you found peace for yourself and are now free. I know as I continue with the next chapter in my life that I will find myself more and more at peace.

I have emailed with your mother and am very pleased and somewhat terrified that she has agreed to meet with me. She even offered me a place to stay in their home. You see, after all this time, I have finally decided it's time to return to Australia. I have never believed in gravesites but Brad, I need to visit yours. I have to. Can it still be denial after all these years and tears? It sounds stupid even when I ask myself. Perhaps it will help to give me some closure so that some of what I call yuk inside can get laid to rest. As for your mom and the rest of your family, I don't know. We had also become quite close in such a short time. I wonder if they blame me like I blame me. I don't know what we will say or how things will be said. I hope to be there in about three months and, Brad, I'm pretty scared. I know some of it will be agonizing and painful and yet I think a lot of good can come from it.

I haven't stopped crying and yet I feel relieved. I feel this has been a long time coming. Parts of me feel numb and parts of me just feel tired.

This sounds pretty stupid, yet again, but I haven't felt your presence for a little while. Are you are busy talking to your grandma, and maybe now my father. I'm certain you are watching over your family. I am also fairly certain that you are keeping tabs on me too. I am open to a friendly reminder, any time. Just sayin'…

I hope you are okay with me writing this book of our story. I know what a kind, gentle soul you were and that you would approve of me reaching out and helping as many people as possible to cope with such a painful turn in life. I don't believe this will cause your family any more pain as I would never want that. Maybe in some small way, they will be brave enough to read this someday. And maybe, just maybe they will find more peace within themselves. I know I have.

Brad, I will continue to work on my hurt and my anger because I know you never meant for this or that you would want to see your loved ones hurting. So, for you and for me, I will continue to work on forgiving you and forgiving me.

Forever and Ever,

Jill, the Cupcake Doolie

XO

(P.S. And I wasn't sure I even had anything to write you…)

DEAR BRAD #1

After deciding to write the above letter, in August of 2017, I purchased a new iPad. While transferring data from one iPad to the other, I came across the following letter to Brad. I wasn't going to share it here, but I found it interesting that I had written it and forgot about it. I also found the comparisons from what I wrote from 2013 to 2017 to be worth sharing as it is similar yet different. Some emotions still seem to be raw and intense. There continue to be so many unanswered questions and all the "what ifs." While the sadness and loneliness still seem strong, the anger doesn't seem so intense. In 2017, I had taken several more steps to come to terms with your death.

June 21, 2013

Dear Brad,

I'm not really sure where to start or what to say. I think it will all come out as I begin.

I'm not sure why tonight, of all nights, that I need to sit down and finally do this. Today is my 46th birthday and soooo many thoughts come to mind. I guess you will never celebrate your 46th birthday, and you're not here to celebrate mine with me. I'm lonely and, right now, I find myself angry at you. I don't want to be but I am. I'm definitely not as angry as often as I used to be, but every once in a while I can't help it. I feel selfish for being angry and that, in itself, makes me more angry. I sometimes think of how things could have been. Would we be here? Would we be there? Would I have joined your business with you? Somehow, I thought for many years that I would have. It seemed right. It seemed to fit. I've pictured us together so many times. I had made it all seem so possible and realistic.

I get angry at myself too! I wish I would have made up my mind a few months sooner. I feel guilty because even though I thought you wanted your space, I should have sent those letters I wrote. I should have emailed and tried calling you more. Maybe you would have told me how you were feeling. Maybe you would have reached out to me. I'm angry I wasn't there for you, and I'm angry at you for not letting me be there for you! I would like to think you would never have done this if only I'd known. I hate the thought of how sad you must have been, how lonely and desperate you must have felt. It tears me up inside to think of you feeling so badly. I can't imagine how you must have felt to do what you did. I am soooo sorry I was not there for you. If only I could change things…

I never stopped loving you or caring for you. I still think of you so often. Last weekend I went camping and was reminded of when we went camping. Today, when I was driving, I was reminded of when we were in the car crash. I was just telling someone about the best year of my life when I went travelling to Australia. I listen to the Eagles' "Peaceful Easy Feeling" and I'm reminded of you playing your guitar and singing to me on the beach. Someone showed me a "dolphin cake," and I was reminded of the time when I went with you and your family down the beach in the Jeep. I had to get out and run with the dolphins. This is all in the last week. No wonder I needed to write this tonight. As hard as it is, I am going to have to start and try to let you go more. I need to heal more and start to move forward. I don't want to be lonely anymore. It has been way too many years (and yet again, why didn't I say something sooner??). I know I can't change what I did or didn't *do, and I can't be angry and so sad. It's not healthy, and I know it's not what you would have wanted.*

I am glad you found peace, I'm really sorry about how you felt it had to happen. The fact that you are now at peace does help me find comfort. I will continue to work on accepting everything that has happened. I truly believe that everything happens for a reason and maybe this book is it; I'm not sure yet.

I don't want to say goodbye, but I really need to start moving forward again…

Forever in my heart,

me

TAKE CARE OF YOU
Some options to Consider

Taking care of yourself is so important, especially when having to cope with some of the curve balls that life throws our way. Working towards a life worth living, whatever that looks like for you, is paramount. Look after yourself when you are not well, rest well, eat well, and get enough exercise. Do things that make you happy and when you are not, spend time with yourself to feel better.

I thank you for reading these stories and letters. I trust that the words have resonated with you, and, if so, inspired you to continue your healing journey.

I have included some resources and suggestions if you think you might need some extra support to assist you with your healing.

AND SO IT CONTINUES...

Since Brads death and my endeavour to write and publish this book, I have gotten divorced, sold the acreage, house sat for many months, travelled to South Africa for seven weeks, dated a few men, paid off a mortgage on my own, and changed careers. Never in a million years would I have thought I would be 50 years old and living on my own. I guess you could say that coping with Brad's death has gotten somewhat less emotional for me. I will never say it has gotten easier.

So many things got in the way through the years preventing the completion of this book sooner: my emotions, lack of literary and technological skills, and just not knowing how to put it all together. Mostly, I have enjoyed this journey I undertook so many years ago. The struggles, the setbacks, and the emotional roller coaster ride were all necessary parts of my healing journey. This book has been a cloud over me for the last several years, and I am very grateful for all of my friends, family and that one person (who came into my life if but for this reason alone) who encouraged me to continue with this endeavor. I am a much stronger person inside. My skills as a counsellor have improved. I am better able to understand and comprehend when others tell me of the struggles in their lives. I understand that life can be really hard sometimes and that we were not meant to struggle through it alone. While I still miss Brad and struggle with the unanswered questions, the completion of this book has provided me with some more closure. My plan is to shift the main focus in my life back to me and my next chapter, whatever that may be. As they say, when one door closes, another door opens!

WHAT YOU CAN DO FOR YOU: AVAILABLE RESOURCES FOR THOSE LEFT BEHIND (SURVIVORS)

Throughout my searching, I have found several resources to be helpful. The prevalence of suicide is steadily increasing around the world and, thankfully, so, too, are supports and resources. What follows is a mere sampling of the resources available to those in search of such support. While the Canadian provinces and/or cities that I have mentioned may not be near you, I found the information contained in these regional websites to be quite valuable and useful.

Accordingly, because Brad lived in Australia, I wanted to include some resources available there as well. The information I have included contains excellent supportive information, regardless of where you currently live.

Canadian resources include:

CANADIAN MENTAL HEALTH ASSOCIATION (CMHA) – I found the Toronto CMHA website particularly helpful. It specifically mentions "Grief after Suicide," which talks about bereavement and stages of grief. We must remember that everyone grieves in their own way, and there is no right or wrong way. The Calgary CMHA developed "Hope and Healing – A

Practical Guide for Survivors of Suicide." This resource talks about various steps of grief and what one might experience after the loss of a loved one to suicide. It has other resources listed as well.

CANADIAN ASSOCIATION FOR SUICIDE PREVENTION (CASP) – This website touches on suicide grief. There is a list of possible reactions and coping strategies.

If you look up the words "hope and healing," you may find as I did that several Canadian articles come up that are informative.

Australian resources include:

SUICIDE CALLBACK SERVICE offers a 24-hour helpline for any concerns related to a potential suicide or if you have lost someone to suicide. The callback service lists helpful articles with headings such as "Common Experiences with Suicide Bereavement," "Looking After Yourself after a Bereavement," "Who Can I Talk to? Supporting Children Bereaved by Suicide," "Supporting Adolescents Bereaved by Suicide" and "Legal Considerations Following a Suicide."

LIFELINE links to crisis support and suicide prevention services. Of note on this website is a 32- page, PDF version of *Survivors of Suicide Booklet – Coping with the Suicide of a Loved One* that you can download and print.

ROSES IN THE OCEAN is an interesting website as it offers various alternatives to facts and suggestions. Under Resources, the first line states that Australia lost 3027 lives to suicide in 2015. Various resources are listed. One is titled "Conversations Matter" and is "To Those Bereaved by Suicide," which includes a fact sheet. Several podcasts share stories of survivors who have lost loved ones to suicide. They share their struggles and suggestions on how to talk about some of the aftereffects of suicide. While the vision of many podcasts is to prevent suicide, they believe that talking openly and sharing past stories is beneficial.

SUPPORT AFTER SUICIDE is a resource that is specifically designed to assist those people who have been bereaved by suicide. They offer counselling and group support as well as having a community that brings together people bereaved by suicide. Included are stories from people who have lost loved ones to suicide.

WRITING A THERAPEUTIC LETTER

Many articles I've read support the value in writing a therapeutic letter to a loved one who has passed away. I know for myself and the individuals included in this book, writing a letter was beneficial. It is a way for you to process, acknowledge and, perhaps, even let go of some of the feelings you harbor. Keeping these feelings inside can manifest and cause long-term suffering, both mentally and physically.

The intentions are to be as honest and open as you possibly can. Write about all the feelings you have experienced and continue to experience as a result of someone's suicide. It may benefit you to pick a time when you can be alone with your thoughts. You may choose to have a friend close by or a phone call away so that you are able to talk with someone you trust.

You do not need to show anyone your letter. In fact, many therapists suggest that you do not keep the letter but destroy it. Destroying it can be a part of the healing process as it signifies letting go of the pain.

Many articles on the internet regard the process of writing a therapeutic letter. I encourage you to read some and pick the one that resonates with you.

Good luck!

SUICIDE IN CANADA
Statistical Information

Highlights

In 2009, there were 3,890 suicides in Canada, a rate of 11.5 per 100,000 people. The suicide rate for males was three times higher than the rate for females.

Although suicide deaths affect almost all age groups, those aged 40 to 59 had the highest rates. Married people had a lower suicide rate than those who were single, divorced or widowed.

Suicide is a preventable death. It is estimated that in 2009 alone, there were about 100,000 years of potential life lost to Canadians under the age of 75 from suicides.

Research shows that mental illness is the most important risk factor for suicide and that more than 90% of people who commit suicide have a mental or addictive disorder.

Depression is the most common illness among those who die from suicide, with approximately 60% suffering from this condition.

No single determinant, including mental illness, is enough on its own to cause suicide. Rather, suicide typically results from the interaction of many factors such as mental illness, marital breakdown, financial hardship, deteriorating physical health, a major loss or a lack of social support.

Males commit suicide at a higher rate than females

In 2009, there were approximately 238,000 deaths in Canada, of which 3,890 were attributed to suicides. During that year, a total of 2,989 males committed suicide compared to 901 females.

It is estimated that for every completed suicide, there are as many as 20 attempts. Males are more likely to die from suicide, but females are three to four times more likely to attempt it. This discrepancy may be due to females using preferable methods, such as poisoning, whereas males tend to use more violent methods such as hanging and firearms.

The highest rates of suicide occur during mid-life

When suicide deaths are examined across age groups, persons aged 40 to 59 have the highest rates. Forty-five percent of all suicides in 2009 were in this age group, compared with 35% for those aged 15 to 39, and 19% for those over the age of 60.

Suicide is a leading cause of death in young people

In 2009, suicide ranked as the ninth leading cause of death in Canada. Among those aged 15 to 34, suicide was the second leading cause of death, preceded only by accidents (unintentional injuries).

Married people are the least likely to commit suicide

For both men and women, married people were the least likely group to commit suicide. Single (never married) people were the most likely at a rate 3.3 times higher, followed by those widowed and divorced. Single men were much more likely to die from suicide than those who were married. Among women, widows had the highest rates of suicide.

Summary

Statistics Canada explores different aspects of suicide in Canada and have shown that males are far more likely to commit suicide than females. Looking at suicides by age group for both sexes, the highest suicide rates were found in those aged 40 to 59. However, suicide ranks second as a leading cause of death for people aged 15 to 34. Looking at suicide deaths by marital status revealed significantly lower rates for married people and a compelling parallel between historical trends for suicide and divorce.

Reference

T. Navaneelan. 2012. Suicide Rates: An Overview. Health at a Glance. Catalogue no. 82-624-X 2012001. https://www150.statcan.gc.ca/n1/pub/82-624-x/2012001/article/11696-eng.htm

BIO

Jill Balacko has dedicated her life to working in careers within the helping professions. She currently works as a behavioural counsellor. Jill lost a very dear friend to suicide and, more recently, her father.

To contact Jill: underthedark@mail.com